LUDWIG VA

M000166185

CONCERTO No. 5

for Piano and Orchestra
E♭ major/Es-Dur/Mi♭ majeur
Op. 73
"Emperor"
Edited by/Herausgegeben von
Paul Badura-Skoda/Akira Imai

P-υ!+1

XIV
18
195

Ernst Eulenburg Ltd
London · Mainz · Madrid · New York · Paris · Tokyo · Toronto · Zürich

CONTENTS/INHALT

Reduction for 2 pianos/Ausgabe für 2 Klaviere
Schott ED 12648

© 2000 Ernst Eulenburg & Co GmbH, Mainz
for Europe excluding the British Isles
Ernst Eulenburg Ltd, London
for all other countries

All rights reserved.
No part of this publication may be reproduced, stored in a retrieval system,
or transmitted in any form or by any means,
electronic, mechanical, photocopying, recording or otherwise,
without the prior written permission of the publisher:

Ernst Eulenburg Ltd
48 Great Marlborough Street
London W1V 2BN

PREFACE/VORWORT

Beethoven composed the E flat major concerto in 1809. It was published in Leipzig in February 1811 by Breitkopf & Härtel, who also produced an improved titled edition during the same year. In November 1810, however, the firm of Clementi & Co. had already published this concerto in London before the publication of the first German edition. The work is dedicated to the Austrian Archduke Rudolph who was Beethoven's pupil, friend and patron.

The première took place at the seventh of the Leipzig Gewandhaus Concerts on 28 November 1811 conducted by Johann Philipp Schulz (1773–1827) with Friedrich Schneider (1786–1853) as soloist and given an enthusiastic review by the music critic Friedrich Rochlitz (1769–1842) in the *Allgemeine musikalische Zeitung*.[1] The first performance in Vienna was on 12 February 1812 by Beethoven's pupil Carl Czerny (1791–1857), whose valuable comments regarding the performance were published in Vol. 4 of his great Piano Tutor, Op. 500.[2] Ten years later Charles Neate (1784–1877) gave the first performance in England. It was not, however, until the period 1830–1840 that the concerto, acclaimed as Beethoven's greatest, was made popular by Franz Liszt (1811–1886) and Ferdinand Hiller (1811–1855). Theodore Döhler (1814–1856) was the first to perform the work in New York in 1855.

The now commonly used title 'Emperor Concerto', possibly invented by Johann Baptist Cramer (1771–1858), probably appeared in England during the 1840s, after Beethoven's death in 1827. It has nothing to

Beethoven komponierte das Es-Dur Klavierkonzert im Jahr 1809. Es erschien im Februar 1811 bei Breitkopf & Härtel, Leipzig, und noch im gleichen Jahr daselbst in einer verbesserten Titelauflage. Doch noch früher als die deutsche Erstausgabe erschien dieses Konzert in London beim Verlag Clementi & Co., nämlich im November 1810. Das Werk ist Beethovens Schüler, Freund und Gönner, dem Erzherzog Rudolph von Österreich gewidmet.

Die erste Aufführung erfolgte am 28. November 1811 im siebten Gewandhauskonzert in Leipzig durch Friedrich Schneider (1786–1853) unter der Leitung von Johann Philipp Schulz (1773–1827) und fand eine begeisterte Kritik von Rochlitz (1769–1842) in der *Allgemeinen musikalischen Zeitung*[1]. Die erste Wiener Aufführung erfolgte etwas später, am 12. Februar 1812 durch Beethovens Schüler Carl Czerny (1791–1857), der später im vierten Band seiner großen Klavierschule op. 500[2] wertvolle Hinweise zur Aufführung veröffentlichte. Die erste englische Aufführung erfolgte 10 Jahre später durch Charles Neate (1784–1877). Doch erst 1830–1840 wurde dieses größte Klavierkonzert Beethovens durch Franz Liszt (1811–1886) und Ferdinand Hiller (1811–1855) populär. In New York wurde es 1855 durch Theodor Döhler (1814–1856) zum ersten Mal aufgeführt.

Der heute übliche Titel „Emperor-Concerto" kam erst nach Beethovens Tod (1827) in Umlauf und dürfte in den 40er Jahren des 19. Jahrhunderts in England aufgekommen sein, möglicherweise durch

---

[1] Leipzig, XIX, 8
[2] Carl Czerny, *Vollständige theoretisch praktische Pianoforte-Schule*, Op. 500, Part 4: *Die Kunst des Vortrags* (Wien, 1842), pp. 114–116; (London: Cock, 1845), pp. 112–114

[1] Leipzig, XIX, 8
[2] Carl Czerny, *Vollständige theoretisch praktische Pianoforte-Schule*, op. 500, Part 4: *Die Kunst des Vortrags*, Wien 1842, S. 114–116. Auch in: Carl Czerny, *Über den richtigen Vortrag der sämtlichen Beethovenschen Klavierwerke*, P. Badura-Skoda (Hrsg.), Wien 1963, S. 106

do with an emperor, least of all Napoleon, of whose high-handed coronation Beethoven disapproved so strongly that he withdrew the dedication from the 'Eroica' Symphony. Rather, the title refers to the generous conception, the majestic 'imperial' gesture, particularly in the first movement, and the triumphal character of both outer movements to which the almost religious, deeply emotional middle movement provides a strong contrast – a contrast not without its own motivation. In the first movement the most tender pianissimo counter-themes contrast with the dense sonority of the main subject, and the B-major key of the second movement is also anticipated, albeit in the enharmonic guise of C flat major (bb159 and 304ff.).

After the gentle fading away of the Adagio, the *attacca* of the third movement is a 'coup de théâtre' which may still have a startling effect on some inattentive listeners today (could Haydn's 'Surprise' Symphony have been an influence here?). It is also worth mentioning that Beethoven's 'heroic period' between 1803 and 1809 seems to have come to an end with this concerto. Among the sketches there are entries like 'Auf die Schlacht Jubelgesang' ('to the battle, song of jubilation') and 'Angriff–Sieg' ('attack, victory'). Here, and in earlier heroic works like the Third and Fifth Symphonies, the 'battle' concept appears in a sublimated form. While soloist and orchestra confront each other more than once in 'fighting spirit', this contrast is overcome and resolved in a sphere of exalted harmony.

The historical aspect of Beethoven's concertos is summarized thus by Basil Deane:

> Beethoven's contribution to the concerto was of outstanding importance. He started with the Mozartian concept of co-operative interplay between soloist

Johann Baptist Cramer (1771–1858). Er hat nichts mit einem Kaiser zu tun, schon gar nicht mit Napoleon, dessen selbst arrangierte Kaiserkrönung Beethoven so mißfiel, daß er die Widmung der Eroica-Symphonie rückgängig machte. Der Titel bezieht sich vielmehr auf die Größe der Konzeption, die majestätische „imperiale" Geste, speziell im I. Satz, und den triumphalen Charakter der Ecksätze, zu denen der quasi religiöse verinnerlichte Mittelsatz einen starken Kontrast bildet. Dieser Gegensatz erscheint aber nicht unmotiviert. Schon im I. Satz finden sich neben den Klangballungen des Hauptthemas zarteste Gegenthemen im Pianissimo, und die Tonart H-Dur des II. Satzes wird schon im I. Satz durch die (enharmonisch gleichen) Ces-Dur-Stellen T. 159 und 304 ff. vorbereitet.

Der plötzliche Beginn des III. Satzes nach dem zartesten Verklingen des Adagio ist ein „Coup de théâtre", der auch heute noch manchen verschlafenen Zuhörer aufschrecken läßt. (Ob da Haydns „Surprise-Symphony" Pate gestanden hat?) Bemerkenswert ist noch, daß dieses Konzert Beethovens „heroische Periode" der Jahre 1803–1809 abzuschließen scheint. Zwischen den Skizzen finden sich Eintragungen wie „Auf die Schlacht Jubelgesang", „Angriff–Sieg". Freilich ist ebenso wie in den vorhergehenden heroischen Werken wie der 3. oder 5. Symphonie die Idee des Kampfes sublimiert. Wenn Solist und Orchester auch mehr als einmal „kämpferisch" einander gegenübertreten, so wird dieser Gegensatz doch in einer höheren Harmonie überwunden und aufgelöst.

Sehr schön schreibt Basil Deane über die historische Stellung der Beethoven-Konzerte:

> „Beethovens Beitrag zum Konzert war von höchster Bedeutung. Er begann mit dem Mozartischen Konzept eines zusammenwirkenden Wechselspiels zwi-

and orchestra in the thematic presentation, adapted it to his own particular kind of dramatic symphonic expression, and finally made of the concerto a vehicle for extreme virtuosity, without in any way detracting from its musical content or lessening the importance of the orchestra. He arrived at a more open conception of the first movement, with early participation of the soloist. He sought, and found, alternatives to the 'set-form' slow movement. He related his movements to each other, not only by linking passages between movements but also by interrelated tonal events. He left a legacy which influenced profoundly, both for good and bad, his 19th-century successors.[3]

The present edition of the Piano Concerto in E flat major represents a first attempt since Beethoven's times at re-establishing the original text (Urtext) according to Beethoven's intentions. Why, one may ask, were so many mistakes in the original edition, as well as in later printed scores based on this edition? The answer reveals an interesting aspect of the relations between Beethoven and his publishers.

During composition of the work the relations between Beethoven and Breitkopf & Härtel in Leipzig (who were publishing his major works at the time) were good, even friendly. Their collaboration took the following form: Beethoven checked the professionally prepared MS copies of his works and then sent them to Leipzig, keeping the autographs in Vienna. In spite of Beethoven's repeated requests, the publishers never let him have proofs and printed such

schen Solist und Orchester in der thematischen Darstellung, eignet sich das Konzert in seiner eigenen Art des dramatischen und symphonischen Ausdrucks an, und macht es schließlich zu einem Träger äußerster Virtuosität, ohne jedoch dabei von seinem musikalischen Inhalt abzulenken oder die Bedeutung des Orchesters zu verändern. Er erreichte ein offeneres Konzept des I. Satzes, bei dem der Solist früher eintreten konnte. Er suchte und fand Alternativen zur festgelegten Form des langsamen Satzes und er verknüpfte Sätze miteinander, nicht nur durch verbindende Motive, sondern auch durch tonale Verwandtschaften. Er hinterließ so ein Erbe, das im Guten wie im Schlechten seine Nachfolger im 19. Jahrhundert tief beinflußte."[3]

Die vorliegende Ausgabe des Es-Dur Klavierkonzerts unternimmt den Versuch, zum ersten Mal seit Beethovens Zeiten den Urtext im Sinne Beethovens wiederherzustellen. Wie war es eigentlich zu den Fehlern in der Originalausgabe und in den darauf fußenden späteren Partiturdrucken gekommen? Die Antwort auf diese Frage wirft ein interessantes Licht auf Beethovens Verhältnis zu seinen Verlegern.

Zur Zeit der Komposition dieses Werkes stand Beethoven in guter, nahezu freundschaftlicher Beziehung zum Leipziger Verlagshaus Breitkopf & Härtel, das damals seine wichtigsten Werke veröffentlichte. Die Zusammenarbeit vollzog sich so, daß Beethoven von ihm selbst überprüfte Abschriften seiner Werke nach Leipzig sandte und seine Autographe in Wien behielt. Trotz wiederholter Mahnungen Beethovens schickte der Verleger ihm keine Korrek-

[3] *The Beethoven Companion/The Beethoven Reader*, ed. D. Arnold and N. Fortune (London/New York, 1971), p. 328

[3] In: D. Arnold und N. Fortune (Hrsg.), *The Beethoven Companion/The Beethoven Reader*, London/New York 1971, S. 328

works rather quickly after they had been checked by the publisher's own proof-readers. Almost inevitably this procedure led to mistakes in the original editions that were never accepted by Beethoven without protest:

26 July 1809: 'Meanwhile, herewith a generous portion of mistakes (regarding the Cello Sonata), to which my attention was drawn by a good friend because I can no longer be bothered with what I have already written. I will arrange the compilation and printing of this list here and have it announced in the papers, so that it can be obtained by all those who have already bought the work. This is further proof that, in my experience, what is printed from manuscripts written in my own hand appears mostly correct in the engravings. Presumably there will also be a number of mistakes in the copy you have because, even if it is looked over by the author, he will no doubt overlook mistakes.'

2 November 1809: '[...] regarding the very beautiful edition, I have to reproach you most emphatically: why is it not free from mistakes??? Why not first a copy for checking for which I have asked repeatedly? Mistakes tend to creep into every copy but they can be corrected by any competent proof-reader [...] I am somehow rather angry about that.'

21 August 1810 'I have also found the following mistake in the C minor Symphony, in the third movement in 3/4 time, when the major ♮ returns to the minor, and where it appears in the bass part as follows:

turabzüge, sondern brachte die Werke nach Lesung einer Hauskorrektur ziemlich schnell im Druck heraus. Dieses Verfahren mußte fast zwangsläufig zu Fehlern in den Original-Ausgaben führen, die Beethoven keineswegs stillschweigend hinnahm:

26. Juli 1809: „Hier eine gute Portion Druckfehler, auf die ich, da ich mich mein Leben nicht mehr bekümmere um das, was ich schon geschrieben habe, durch einen guten Freund von mir aufmerksam gemacht wurde (nämlich in der Violoncell-Sonate). Ich lasse hier dieses Verzeichnis schreiben und drukken und in der Zeitung ankündigen, daß alle diejenigen, welche sie schon gekauft, dieses holen können. Dieses bringt mich wieder auf die Bestätigung der von mir gemachten Erfahrung, daß nach meinen von meiner eigenen Handschrift geschriebenen Sachen am richtigsten gestochen wird. Vermutlich dürften sich auch in der Abschrift, die Sie haben, manche Fehler finden; aber bei dem Übersehen übersieht wirklich der Verfasser die Fehler."

2. November 1809: „[...] ich mache Ihnen recht lebhafte Vorwürfe, warum die sehr schöne Auflage nicht ohne Inkorrektheit??? Warum nicht erst ein Exemplar zur Übersicht, wie ich schon oft verlangte? In jede Abschrift schleichen sich Fehler ein, die aber ein jeder geschickte Korrektor [beim Verlag, Anm. d. Verf.] verbessern kann [...] Etwas sehr ärgerlich bin ich deswegen."

21. August 1810: „Folgende Fehler habe ich noch in der Sinfonie aus C moll gefunden, nämlich im 3ten Stück im 3/4 Takt, wo nach dem dur ♮ wieder das moll eintritt, steht so: ich nehme gleich die Baßstimme, nämlich:

The two crossed out bars are two bars too many and must be cut, of course also in all other parts which have rests.'

Beethoven reminded Breitkopf of the same mistake on 15 October 1810, asking whether the two superfluous bars in the third movement of the symphony had been eliminated. 'Perhaps I forgot to answer your letter, and therefore the bars might still be there.'

If Beethoven had not expressly demanded this correction, these two superfluous and musically pointless bars in the Fifth Symphony might still be played today. They were indeed never cut in the edition of the parts, printed 15 months earlier, and were included, in spite of Beethoven's two letters, in the score which Breitkopf & Härtel published in 1826. The definitive correction was finally made by Mendelssohn on the occasion of the Lower Rhine Musical Festival in Aachen, 1846.[4]

c. 2 May 1811: 'In the [Fifth Piano] K [Concerto] there are rather a lot of mistakes.'

6 May 1811: 'Mistakes – mistakes! You yourself are nothing but one big mistake! I shall have to send you my copyist, I must come myself, if I don't intend my works – published just as a mass of mistakes. The music tribunal in Leipzig does not apparently produce one single decent

Die zwei Takte, worüber das x ist, sind zu viel und müssen ausgestrichen werden, versteht sich auch in allen übrigen Stimmen, die pausieren."

Am 15. Oktober 1810 erinnerte Beethoven Breitkopf an denselben Fehler und fragte, ob die beiden überzähligen Takte im III. Satz der Symphonie schon ausgeschieden seien. „Vielleicht vergaß ich, Ihnen zu antworten, und die Takte könnten noch da sein."

Hätte Beethoven diese Korrektur nicht ausdrücklich verlangt, so würde die 5. Symphonie wohl noch heute mit diesen zwei überzähligen, musikalisch unsinnigen Takten erklingen. Sie wurden nämlich in der eineinviertel Jahre vorher gedruckten Stimmenausgabe nicht nachträglich ausgemerzt und sind trotz der beiden Briefe Beethovens in die bei Breitkopf & Härtel 1826 erschienene Partitur aufgenommen worden. Die endgültige Richtigstellung erfolgte erst 1846 durch Mendelssohn anläßlich des Niederrheinischen Musikfestes in Aachen.[4]

Ca. 2. Mai 1811: „Im [5. Klavier-] K[onzert] sind ziemlich viele Fehler."

6. Mai 1811: „Fehler – Fehler! Sie sind selbst ein einziger Fehler! Da muß ich meinen Copisten hinschicken, dort muß ich selbst hin, wenn ich will, daß meine Werke – nicht als bloße Fehler erscheinen. Das Musik-Tribunal in Leipzig bringt, wie es scheint, nicht einen einzigen or-

[4] See A.W. Thayer, *Ludwig van Beethovens Leben*, rev. E. Forbes as *Thayers Life of Beethoven* (Princeton, 1964), Vol. 1, pp. 500f.

[4] Vgl. A.W. Thayer, *Ludwig van Beethovens Leben*, übersetzt v. H. Deiters, hrsg. v. H. Rieman, Bd. 1, Leipzig[3-5] 1923, S. 95 f.

proof-reader, and you send the works away even before you have received the corrected proof.'[5]

Beethoven's list of corrections for the Fifth Piano Concerto was rediscovered in 1983 at auction by Sotheby's, London. This also explains why Breitkopf & Härtel published a new edition relatively quickly. While it is not substantially different in appearance (title-page, for instance), there are numerous corrections in the piano part which were evidently made directly onto the plates.[6] That only Beethoven could have made these corrections is evident from the fact that many of those in the new edition were based on the autograph score.

Of particular interest are corrections in this new edition at places where even the autograph has mistakes or inaccuracies. For instance, in the first movement, b371, Beethoven had forgotten to add in the score the sign for lifting the pedal, as well as the ottava sign in b465 where it is musically necessary.

For quite some time Beethoven was unable to make up his mind regarding the tempo indication for the third movement. The autograph score bears the indication 'Rondo Allegro', followed by the words 'non tanto', crossed out in pencil. This

dentlichen Korrektor hervor; dabei schicken Sie, noch ehe sie die Korrektur erhalten die Werke ab."[5]

Erst 1983 ist Beethovens Korrekturliste zum 5. Klavierkonzert bei einer Versteigerung im Auktionshaus Sotheby in London aufgetaucht. So ist es erklärlich, daß Breitkopf & Härtel relativ bald eine Neuauflage herausbrachte, die sich zwar äußerlich (z. B. im Titelblatt) nicht von der fehlerhaften ersten Auflage der Originalausgabe unterschied, jedoch im Klavierpart zahlreiche Korrekturen aufwies, die offensichtlich in den Stichplatten vorgenommen wurden.[6] Daß der Urheber dieser Korrekturen nur Beethoven selbst sein konnte, erkennt man daran, daß die Neuauflage an vielen Stellen im Sinne des Partiturautographs verbessert wurde.

Von besonderem Interesse sind die Verbesserungen dieser Neuauflage an jenen Stellen, wo selbst das Autograph fehlerhaft oder ungenau ist. So hatte Beethoven im I. Satz das Pedalaufhebungszeichen in T. 371 versehentlich nicht in der Partitur notiert und in T. 465 das musikalisch notwendige *8va*-Zeichen niederzuschreiben vergessen.

Beim Beginn des III. Satzes hat Beethoven längere Zeit in Bezug auf die Tempobezeichnungen geschwankt: Im Partiturautograph steht „Rondo Allegro", dahinter die Worte „non tanto", mit Bleistift durchgestrichen. Die erste Ausgabe hat

---

[5] A possible explanation for this seemingly inexplicable behaviour of the publisher could be due to the postal conditions prevalent at the time; the sending and returning of proof material would have resulted in a delay of two months in the publication of a work by Beethoven. Furthermore, Breitkopf had to fear pirate editions, caused by indiscretion in Vienna, and that would have damaged him considerably.

[6] Piano concertos and symphonies were, at that time, usually published in sets of parts; printed full scores were rare exceptions.

[5] Für dieses (uns) heute unerklärlich scheinende Verhalten des Verlegers gibt es folgende mögliche Erklärung: Bei den damaligen Postverhältnissen hätte das Hin- und Zurückschicken von Korrekturexemplaren mindestens zu einer zweimonatigen Verzögerung der Herausgabe eines Beethovenschen Werkes geführt. Vor allem aber mußte Breitkopf befürchten, daß dann durch Indiskretion in Wien Raubdrucke entstehen könnten, durch die sein Verlag empfindlich geschädigt worden wäre.

[6] Bekanntlich erschienen damals Klavierkonzerte und Symphonien gewöhnlich in Einzelstimmen; Partiturdrucke waren eine seltene Ausnahme.

would explain why the tempo indication in the first edition is only 'Allegro'. Beethoven's final decision was, after all, for a more moderate tempo, hence the indication 'allegro ma non troppo' in the corrected edition, and also in the Collected Works edition (c.1870). Because of lack of space, however, the words 'ma non troppo' are printed in the second edition not directly after the word 'Allegro' but closer to the 'ff' indication ('fortissimo ma non troppo' would be contradictory). Since Beethoven wrote pedal indications *between* the two piano staves, the word 'Pedal' was often printed erroneously as 'pia:'. This also happened in the new edition (and many later editions) as, for instance, in the first movement, bb162 and 420, and in the third movement, b144. (The p in the third movement of many editions, bb402 and 404, is not shown in any of the sources and does not make sense. The varied tutti, bb398–402, demands a f followed by a diminuendo.)

A comparison between the first and second editions of the original publication seems to suggest that Beethoven corrected only the piano part. This is a reasonable assumption if one considers that correcting individual orchestral parts is a very laborious, time consuming task, and that Beethoven was mainly concerned with the correct reproduction of the piano part. Thus it became more likely that various mistakes in the orchestra were to remain uncorrected to the present time, as has been mentioned earlier. Although Wilhelm Altmann corrected a few errors in his 1933 revision of this score, he unfortunately left a great number of sometimes grave mistakes untouched. What he described in his Critical Commentary as 'easier versions' of the piano part are really no more than adjustments caused by the limited range of many contemporary pianos which did not go beyond c''''. That even f'''' was not high enough for Beethoven is

deshalb als Tempoangabe bloß „Allegro". Schließlich entschied Beethoven sich doch für ein gemäßigtes Tempo und ließ in den verbesserten Auflagen die Bezeichnung „allegro ma non troppo" drucken, die auch von der späteren Gesamtausgabe übernommen wurde. Aus Raummangel stehen die Worte „ma non troppo" in der 2. Auflage übrigens nicht direkt hinter dem Wort „Allegro", sondern näher an der Bezeichnung ff. (Ein „fortissimo ma non troppo" wäre aber widersinnig). Da Beethoven seine Pedalbezeichnungen zwischen den beiden Systemen zu notieren pflegte, wurde so manches „Pedal" irrtümlich als „pia:" wiedergegeben, auch in der Neuauflage und vielen späteren Ausgaben. Dies bezieht sich u.a. auf den I. Satz T. 162, T. 420 und auf den III. Satz T. 144. (Das in vielen Ausgaben stehende p im III. Satz T. 402 und 404 steht überhaupt in keiner Quelle und ist sinnwidrig: Die variierte Wiederholung des Tutti T. 398–402 erfordert ein f mit nachfolgendem diminuendo.)

Wie der Vergleich der 1. und 2. Auflage der Originalausgabe zeigt, scheint Beethoven nur die Klavierstimme korrigiert zu haben. Dies ist verständlich, wenn man bedenkt, daß das Verbessern einzelner Orchesterstimmen äußerst mühsam und zeitraubend ist, und daß es Beethoven vor allem auf eine korrekte Wiedergabe des Soloparts ankam. – So kam es eher dazu, daß mehrere Fehler im Orchester bis zum heutigen Tag unkorrigiert geblieben waren, wie eingangs bemerkt wurde. Zwar hat Wilhelm Altmann bei seiner Revision dieser Partitur 1933 einige wenige Stellen verbessert, jedoch leider eine ganze Anzahl zum Teil gravierender Fehler stehengelassen. Was er im Revisionsbericht als „Erleichterungen" der Klavierstimme bezeichnet, waren in Wirklichkeit Anpassungen an den beschränkten Tonumfang vieler damaliger Klaviere, die nicht über das viergestrichene c hinausgingen. Daß Beet-

proved by bb332–333 in the first movement. In this passage Beethoven had originally taken the octave passage up to the high g″″ but then crossed out the last two of the high notes, presumably 'rather by necessity than by virtue'.

In the present edition the piano part is printed also in the tutti passages, since this is the way in which it appears in both the autograph and the German first edition. Beethoven clearly differentiates between the large notes, and the small cue notes which indicate the entries of the various instruments. This kind of notation served as a substitute for a full score at a time when the publication of such scores, or versions for two pianos, had not become common practice. Since these notes in small print were surely not meant to be played, they are not reproduced in the present edition. With regard to the bass notes in large print, however, it can be assumed that Beethoven intended, at least in this concerto, that the piano should participate in the tutti passages by playing a kind of continuo part similar to those in Mozart's piano concertos. The following points are in support of this assumption:

1. The bass (printed large) of the piano in the tutti passages follows the bass of the strings except when the bass line is passed on to the viola or a wind instrument; in this case it is printed in small notes.

2. The very careful figuring of the bass would hardly make sense if it were not intended as an indication actually to play with the orchestra; this is particularly evi-

hoven selbst das viergestrichene f als Spitzenton nicht genügte, zeigt T. 332–333 des I. Satzes. Hier hatte Beethoven den Oktavenzug in seiner Partitur ursprünglich bis zum hohen g (4) geführt. Da aber kein Klavierinstrument der damaligen Zeit über diesen Tonumfang verfügte, strich er die beiden letzten hohen Noten wieder durch, sicherlich „aus der Not und nicht aus Tugend".

Erstmalig wird in dieser Ausgabe die Klavierstimme auch während der Tutti nach dem Autograph und der deutschen Erstausgabe wiedergegeben. Beethoven unterscheidet darin deutlich zwischen den groß geschriebenen bzw. gedruckten Baßnoten und den kleinen Stichnoten, welche die Einsätze der verschiedenen Instrumente anzeigen. Diese Art der Notierung diente als Partiturersatz in einer Zeit, als es noch nicht üblich war, Partituren oder zweiklavierige Ausgaben von Klavierkonzerten zu drucken. Da diese klein gedruckten Noten sicherlich nicht mitzuspielen sind, wurden sie in der vorliegenden Ausgabe weggelassen. Anders steht es hingegen mit der Generalbaßbezifferung. Es besteht aller Grund anzunehmen, daß Beethoven zumindestens in diesem Konzert mit einem generalbaßartigen Mitspielen des Klavierparts während der Tutti rechnete, ähnlich, wie es bei den Mozart-Klavierkonzerten der Fall war. Folgende Gründe sprechen für diese Annahme:

1. Die (groß notierten) Klavierbässe im Tutti gehen mit den Streicherbässen konform, schweigen aber, wenn die Baßlinie auf die Viola oder ein Blasinstrument übergeht; sie werden dann klein notiert.

2. Die sehr sorgfältige Bezifferung ergäbe kaum einen Sinn, wenn sie nicht zum tatsächlichen Mitspielen notiert worden wäre; dies zeigt sich insbesondere bei den

dent in the numerous 'tasto solo' directions which are known to mean that only the bass line, and not the chords, are to be played.

Nevertheless, there is as yet no definitive answer to the question whether a figured bass was, in Beethoven's time, still realized in the tutti passages of piano concertos. The fact that, during this period, a transition towards the modern practice – a silent solo part in the tutti – had begun, is borne out by the first English edition which appeared before the original German edition of the concerto. There, too, the bass notes are in bold print, and the cue notes are small. However, the figuring of the bass is omitted.[7]

Finally, we wish to extend our sincere thanks to the Staatsbibliothek zu Berlin – Preußischer Kulturbesitz, formerly the Deutsche Staatsbibliothek, for allowing the repeated inspection of Beethoven's autograph MS, and for making a microfilm available. We are equally grateful for the assistance of the staff of the archive of the Musik-Abteilung of the Österreichische Nationalbibliothek, and of the Gesellschaft der Musikfreunde in Vienna.

Paul Badura-Skoda/Akira Imai
Translation Stefan de Haan

zahlreichen „tasto solo"-Notierungen, welche bekanntlich bedeuten, daß an solchen Stellen nur die Baßlinie, aber keine Akkorde zu spielen sind.

Trotzdem ist die Frage, inwieweit zu Beethovens Zeiten noch Generalbaß während der Tutti in den Klavierkonzerten gespielt wurde, nicht eindeutig zu lösen. Daß sich in diese Periode ein Übergang zur modernen Praxis – Schweigen des Soloparts während der Tutti – anbahnte, zeigt die englische Erstausgabe des 5. Klavierkonzertes, die sogar noch vor der deutschen Originalausgabe erschien. Auch dort sind die Baßnoten groß und die Stichnoten klein gedruckt, die Generalbaßbezifferung ist aber weggefallen.[7]

Abschließend möchten wir der Staatsbibliothek zu Berlin – Preußischer Kulturbesitz (früher Deutsche Staatsbibliothek) für die wiederholte Einsichtnahme in Beethovens Autograph und für die Zur-Verfügung-Stellung eines Mikrofilms herzlich danken. Ebenso herzlich sei dem Personal der Musik-Abteilung der Österreichischen Nationalbibliothek und des Archivs der Gesellschaft der Musikfreunde in Wien gedankt.

Paul Badura-Skoda/Akira Imai

---

[7] For a detailed discussion of performance practice for figured bass in Beethoven's piano concertos cf. "Beethoven's Basso Continuo: Notation and Performance" in Robin Stowell ed., *Performing Beethoven*, Cambridge Studies in Performance Practice, (Cambridge 1994). (Review by Paul and Eva Badura-Skoda in *Performance Practice Review* Vol. 10, No. 2, Madison Wisconsin 1977.)

[7] Die Generalbaßpraxis wird ausführlich von Tibor Szasz erläutert in seinem Aufsatz „Beethoven's Basso Continuo: Notation and Performance" in: Robin Stowell (Hrsg.), *Performing Beethoven*, Cambridge Studies in Performance Practice, Cambridge 1994. (Aufsatz rezensiert von Paul und Eva Badura-Skoda in: *Performance Practice Review*, Vol. 10, No. 2, Madison Wisconsin 1977.)

Editorial Notes

Revisionsbericht

The present edition is believed to be the first in attempting to differentiate between staccato strokes (ꞌ) and staccato dots (·), which in Beethoven's autograph are distinct and presumably intentionally so. His basso continuo indications in the solo part are also deliberate, and most of these are reproduced in the main text. There are numerous ossia-versions in the solo part, particularly in the highest ranges of the keyboard, and these were printed in the original editions because many contemporary instruments did not extend above c''''. The ossia are summarized in the report below. Today they are of limited interest except when period instruments are used. The alterations necessarily made by Beethoven are worth mentioning since in some of them the notes are not just transposed down but the lines are changed in an artful manner.

Es wurde in der vorliegenden Ausgabe erstmals versucht, den Unterschied zwischen Staccato-Keilen (ꞌ) und Staccato-Punkten (·) wiederzugeben, die Beethoven wohl mit Absicht im Autograph eintrug. Beabsichtigt waren von ihm auch die „basso continuo" - Eintragungen für den Solopart (siehe Vorwort); sie sind größtenteils im Haupttext wiedergegeben. Ferner die vielen Ossia-Versionen für Klavier in den besonders hohen Lagen, die in den Originalausgaben abgedruckt sind, einfach weil der Tonumfang vieler Instrumente der damaligen Zeit nur bis c4 reichte. Sie sind im Anschluß im detaillierten Revisionsbericht zusammengefaßt dargestellt. Solche aus technischen Gründen notwendigen Abweichungen sind für uns heute weniger interessant, es sei denn man spielt auf historischen Instrumenten. Hierfür notwendige Änderungen Beethovens sind künstlerisch erwähnenswert, denn bei manchen wurden nicht nur die Töne einfach tiefer gesetzt, sondern die musikalischen Linien sind ausgeklügelt geändert worden.

Principal Sources

Hauptquellen

AUT   Autograph full score, Staatsbibliothek zu Berlin – Preußischer Kulturbesitz, Musikabteilung mit Mendelssohn-Archiv, Berlin

AUT   Partitur-Autograph, Staatsbibliothek zu Berlin – Preußischer Kulturbesitz, Musikabteilung mit Mendelssohn-Archiv, Berlin

lED   Piano first edition / engraving, Breitkopf & Härtel, Leipzig, February 1811, plate number 1613. The title-page reads: Grand / CONCERTO / Pour le Pianoforte / avec Accompagnement / de l'Orchestre /composé et dédié / à Son Altesse Imperiale / ROUDOLPHE / Archi-Duc d'Autriche etc. / par / L. v. Beethoven / Priorité des Editeurs / Ouev. 73 — Pr.

lED   Erster Stich der Klavierpartitur in Originalausgabe, Breitkopf & Härtel in Leipzig, Februar 1811 Plattennummer 1613 mit der folgenden Titelseite: Grand / CONCERTO / Pour le Pianoforte / avec Accompagnement / de l'Orchestre / composé et dédié / à Son Altesse Imperiale / ROUDOLPHE / Archi-Duc d' Autriche etc. / par / L. v. Beethoven /

4 Rthlr. / à Leipsic / Chez Breitkopf & Härtel. Copy in the Gesellschaft der Musikfreunde, Vienna.

Priorité des Editeurs / Ouev.73 — Pr. 4 Rthlr. / à Leipsic / Chez Breitkopf & Härtel. Gesellschaft der Musikfreunde, Wien

2ED Piano second edition, based on first engraving, plate number 1613 with corrections specified by Beethoven; cf. preface. Copy in the Nationalbibliothek, Vienna.

2ED Zweite Auflage der Originalausgabe mit den von Beethoven veranlaßten Stichkorrekturen in den Platten (Plattennr. 1613); siehe Vorwort. Nationalbibliothek Wien

ERRATA 'Errata zum Es-Dur Konzert' (Errata in the E flat major Concerto), Beethoven's MS which probably was part of his letter dated 6 May 1811 to Breitkopf & Härtel in Leipzig. In this recently discovered document, which was sold by auction in 1983, Beethoven corrected the printing errors in the solo part of 1ED.

ERRATA „Errata zum Es-Dur Konzert", autographes Manuskript, welches höchstwahrscheinlich zu Beethovens Brief vom 6. Mai 1811 an Breitkopf & Härtel in Leipzig gehört. In diesem 1983 zur Auktion gekommenen, neuentdeckten Dokument verbesserte Beethoven die Stichfehler in der Solostimme in 1ED, siehe Vorwort.

CLEM First English edition published by Clementi & Co., London, November 1810, just before 1ED. The title-page reads: Grand Concerto / for the / PIANO FORTE / As newly constructed / BY CLEMENTI & Co. / with additional Keys up to F. & also arranged for the Piano Forte up to C. / with Accompaniments for a / Full Orchestra / COMPOSED BY / Lewis van Beethoven / Op. 64 [sic] /London, Printed by Clementi & Compy. 26, Cheapside

CLEM Englische Erstausgabe, 1810 von Clementi & Co. in London kurz vor 1ED veröffentlicht. Die Titelseite lautet: Grand Concerto / for the PIANO FORTE / As newly constructed / BY CLEMENTI & Co. / with additional Keys up to F. & also arranged for the Piano Forte up to C. / with Accompaniments for a / Full Orchestra / COMPOSED BY / Lewis van Beethoven / Op. 64 [sic!] / London, Printed by Clementi & Compy. 26, Cheapside

Textual Notes

AUT = Autograph full score
1ED = 1st piano edition
2ED = 2nd piano edition
ERRATA = Beethoven's letter of 6 May 1811
CLEM = 1st English edition

Pfte = Solo pianoforte
Str = Strings
Ww = Woodwind
Orch = Orchestra
b(b) = bar(s)
n(n) = note(s)
strokes = ╻

Slurs for irregular groupings, e.g. quintuplets, sextuplets, etc, conform to the customary notation practice of Beethoven's time. Except for the triplet figures in the first movement main themes they do not signify *legato*.

Mov. I

bar 2   Pfte n7 fingering from AUT, 1ED, 2ED

4   Pfte 1ED, 2ED rh c appears after lh A♭; AUT unclear here but cf alignment following of similar 2 notes 1 and 2 octaves higher

11ff   Str stacc stroke as in AUT

17   Cl1 'Solo' and *dolce* indicate the respective passages here and elsewhere should stand out, be expressive and gentle

73   Vc/Cb stacc stroke on basis of parallel b237

115, 116   Pfte 1ED, 2ED rh:

122   Pfte AUT beat 1 originally    , the slur taken into 1ED over nn1–4;   CLEM beat 1

130   Pfte *p* on basis of Str (unclear in AUT), also *cresc.* in b734

158   Pfte AUT, 1ED, 2ED, CLEM rh nn1–8 ♪♪♪♪♪♪♪♪ (cf b415)

162, 419   Pfte 🎵 correct in CLEM, but 1ED, 2ED shown as *p*

165   Pfte 1ED, 2ED, CLEM rh phrasing ♩♩♩ ♩♩♩♩

174,175,   Pfte fingering from 1ED, 2ED, absent in AUT
177–179

184–185,   Pfte AUT originally phrased ♩♫♫♩♩ but later corrected, these corrections not
188–189 etc.   observed in 1ED, 2ED, CLEM

184ff   Pfte lh stacc dots represent short, thin strokes, rh stacc dots represent thick stacc
strokes above stave in AUT; 1ED, 2ED show all these as stacc strokes; Ww AUT weak
stacc strokes

185   Ww AUT n1 possibly stacc dot

195   Pfte fingering from 1ED, 2ED, not in AUT; AUT n1 *sf* in addition to lh *sforzato*, presumably an error; bb195, 394, 435 CLEM lh n2 *rinf.* instead of *sforzato*, possibly a
later correction by Beethoven in the copy (now lost) supplied for CLEM

225   Pfte fingering from 1ED, 2ED

284   Fl1 AUT b♭″, obviously an error

300   Pfte *cresc.* from CLEM, believed to be a later correction by Beethoven (cf b195
above)

319   Pfte *sempre stacc.* from 1ED, 2ED

321, 322,   VII/II, Vc/Cb stacc strokes in CLEM
325, 326

325   Vc/Cb AUT still has stacc strokes, presumably in error

331   Vc/Cb AUT, 1ED, 2ED nn2–7 stacc strokes

332   Pfte AUT f♯″″ to g″″ written but subsequently deleted, presumably because contemporary instruments (1809) did not encompass these notes

335ff   Pfte in Beethoven's time it was customary for almost all trills to end with a turn

340–341   Pfte 1ED, 2ED, CLEM rh phrase covers only b341, ditto bb345–346

346   Pfte *cresc.* from 1ED, 2ED

357   Vla AUT repeats *cresc.*

371   Pfte pedal release from 2ED; 1ED, 2ED have barline after initial 4 beats, presumably
following original AUT, which had cadenza barlines but were carefully erased; AUT
barline between bb371, 372 missing (erased end of page)

442–424   Cb AUT (beginning of page 53, recto), 1ED, 2ED, CLEM each bar lacking crotchet A♭

422   Pfte slur should reach n5 on basis of b165

423   Pfte 1ED, 2ED pedal release missing

431   Pfte fingering from 1ED, 2ED

441 ff   Pfte AUT rh thick stacc strokes, lh thin stacc strokes; CLEM strokes for both hands

443, 447, 448   Pfte 1ED, 2ED phrasing ♩ 𝄢 (cf bb184–185 above)

446   Pfte 1ED, 2ED *sf* missing

453   Pfte 1ED, 2ED lh n14 b♭ presumably an error; rh nn4–6 staccs from *ossia* version

462   Vc 'uno Violoncello' added on basis of exposition b205; AUT has it in b466

480   Pfte AUT, CLEM no *sempre ped.*

490, 493   Tr 1/2 AUT n1 originally 𝅗𝅥 but later changed; Pfte pedal release from 1ED, 2ED

496   Pfte fn 'Non si fa una Cadenza, ma s'attacca subito il seguente' from 1ED, 2ED

503   Pfte lh fingering from 1ED, 2ED

506–507   Pfte 1ED, 2ED tie missing

522   Cor 1/2 AUT nn3, 4 stacc not clear, possibly ink smudge or fault in paper

534   Fl 1/2 AUT nn1–4 slur

542–553   Pfte 𝄢 b542 from AUT, bb542–553, except b546, in 1ED, 2ED, CLEM

546–550, 552   Pfte AUT, 1ED, 2ED, CLEM lh show ⌣ as ⌣

550–565   Ww, Str from AUT in an unknown hand; Pfte from 1ED, 2ED; AUT these bars lost

563   Pfte CLEM no *pp*; b565 1ED, 2ED b565 no *leggiermente*

577   Pfte CLEM *fff sempre* beginning of bar, '*pedal*' having been omitted, presumably in error; Orch *più f* by analogy with Vl I which is in AUT, the same applies to *ff* in b579

579   Pfte *sempre ped.* from 1ED, 2ED

579, 580   Pfte AUT, CLEM no staccs

Mov. II

1   'Adagio un poco mosso' from CLEM; AUT, 1ED, 2ED 'Adagio un poco moto'; Pfte AUT n3 originally d♯ figured 6

20–22   Pfte 1ED, 2ED, CLEM nn4–6 phrased ♩♩♩

28   Pfte 1ED, 2ED, CLEM rh n9 no accent

33   Pfte 1ED, 2ED single grace-note d″ ♪

45   Pfte, 1ED, 2ED, CLEM rh nn1–4 phrased together

54–55   Pfte rh phrase from AUT

56   Vl II AUT n2

59   Pfte 1ED, 2ED, CLEM rh no accents

73   Vl II n2 a♯ in AUT

79   Pfte 1ED, 2ED pedal release under quaver rest

80   Str AUT n2 clearly pizz. and *p*; other editions frequently print pizz. on n1

82   Pfte 'semplice poco tenuto' and ⌢ from 1ED, 2ED

Mov. III

1   'Allegro ma non troppo' from 2ED; AUT originally 'Allegro non tanto' with 'non tanto' later crossed out by Beethoven; 1ED 'Allegro', CLEM 'Allegro non tanto' (see also Editorial Notes above)

9   (also 13, 102, 106, 254) Pfte *nachdrücklich* (b349 *mit Nachdruck*) in AUT; bb9, 254, 348 *espressivo* between staves from AUT, 1ED, 2ED; CLEM has neither

47, 58   Pfte fingering by analogy with bb292, 293

49   Pfte AUT *dolce* difficult to read, could be 'solo', ditto b294

53, 55   Pfte CLEM no ⟨

58, 60   Pfte AUT, 2ED arpeggiated chords indicated  with similar indications used at bb305, 307; pedal signs by analogy with bb305, 307, but bb58, 60 1ED, 2ED have pedal release signs near beat 2

64   Fg1 AUT nn1–5 phrase

70   Pfte lh/rh slurs from CLEM and on basis of parallel b317, where 1ED, 2ED lh slur is missing

85   Vl I/II stacc strokes by analogy with b84, where AUT has stacc strokes

96–106   AUT not written out but replaced by 'come sopra'

107   Pfte AUT, CLEM *p* missing

142   Pfte 1ED, 2ED *sempre f* missing

144   Pfte fingering from 1ED, 2ED; 1ED, 2ED n1 *p* presumably a mistake (cf Editorial Notes above)

146   Pfte 1ED, 2ED *f* missing

161   Pfte 1ED, 2ED *dolce* missing

211ff   Editorial dynamic suggestions in consideration of the power of a modern grand piano

220	Pfte fingering from AUT, not in 1ED, 2ED
222, 224, 226	Pfte lh stacc stroke from 2ED, ERRATA
223	Pfte *sf* from 1ED, 2ED, CLEM; AUT here not written out but has 'sim.', indicating repeat b232 – with or without *sf*?
238	Pfte all sources have repeated *p*; AUT originally had *p* here but later Beethoven, in emphatic writing, placed the *p* in b236, presumably forgetting to cancel the *p* in b238. A repeated *p* is unlikely for Beethoven since he would always use *sempre p* in such cases.
248–257	AUT not written out but replaced by 'come sopra 10 Takt'
261–281	Aut not written out but has '25 Takte tutti'
289	Pfte 1ED, 2ED *sf* missing
292, 293	Pfte fingering from 1ED, 2ED
298, 300	Pfte CLEM ⟍ missing
301	Pfte 1ED, 2ED *p* ⟨ , the cresc apparently a mistake
314	Orch AUT *f* missing
324	Pfte rh nn6–7 slur from 1ED, 2ED, CLEM
333, 334	Pfte AUT lh stacc dots missing
348	Pfte 1ED, 2ED *p* missing
360	Cb as AUT (some printed editions show nn6, 7 octave higher)
369–369	Fg1 'Solo', *dolce* from AUT
390	Pfte fingering from 1ED, 2ED; Ob, Cl, Cor stacc strokes in AUT
402, 404	Pfte no new dynamic added to these bars in the sources; some editions do so erroneously
419	Pfte AUT originally 'tempo primo' but 'primo allegro' added later by Beethoven in pencil
426	AUT originally Pfte lh e♭/E♭, Vc/Cb e♭, changed by Beethoven in Vc/Cb to B♭, but he omitted similarly to change Pfte

Paul Badura-Skoda/
Akira Imai

Ossia Versions for Piano

Mov. I

bar 163   rh beats 1, 2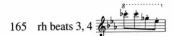

165   rh beats 3, 4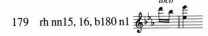

178   rh n1 b♭″

179   rh nn15, 16, b180 n1

206   rh beats 3, 4 octave lower

215   rh beats 3, 4, bb216, 217

274, 275   Alternative

303   Both hands, beats 3, 4, b304 n1 octave lower

332   rh

351–356

391   rh beat 1 octave lower

418   rh beats 1, 2

420–422   rh

434   beat 4, b435 n1

436   beat 4

452, 453   rh

483   rh beat 4, b484 n1

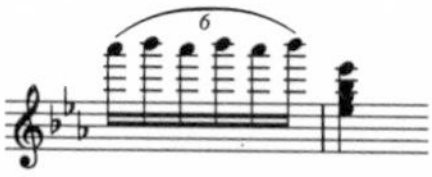

493   rh last 6 notes replaced by

502   rh beats 3, 4, b503 beat 1

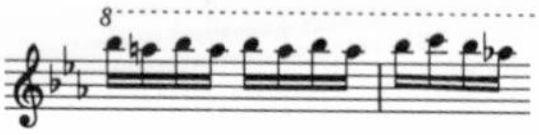

546–553   rh

561–568   rh

572 beat 4–end of mov.

Mov. II

56 rh

Mov. III

134–137

167–170 rh

178–179

206

333 rh beat 1

337, 338

424, 425

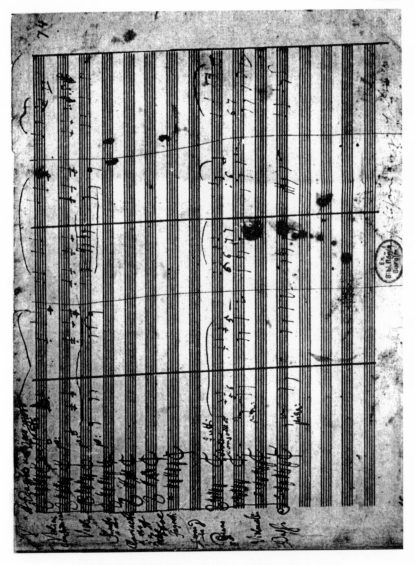

Beethoven, Concerto No. 5, Op. 73, Autograph MS
D-B *Mus. ms. autogr. Beethoven 15. Movement II, fol. 74r, bb1–5*
Preußischer Kulturbesitz Berlin – Musikabteilung mit Mendelssohn-Archiv
Reproduced by permission © bpk

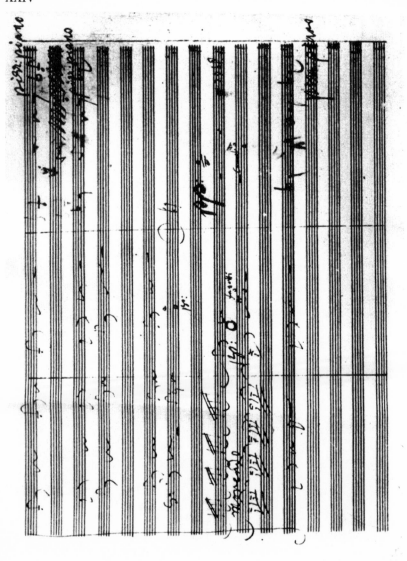

Beethoven, Concerto No. 5, Op. 73, Autograph MS
D-B *Mus. ms. autogr. Beethoven 15. Movement II, fol. 85v, bb78–80*
Preußischer Kulturbesitz Berlin – Musikabteilung mit Mendelssohn-Archiv
Reproduced by permission © bpk

CONCERTO No. 5

Ludwig van Beethoven
(1770–1827)
Op. 73

I. Allegro

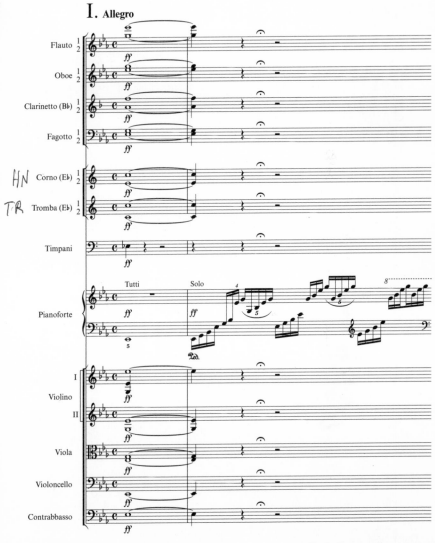

Edited by Paul Badura-Skoda & Akira Imai
© 2000 Ernst Eulenburg & Co GmbH
and Ernst Eulenburg Ltd

4

14

20

EE 6862

24

32

EE 6862

36

38

EE 6862

53

EE 6862

56

58

62

64

EE 6862

66

EE 6862

93

EE 6862

94

NB *Non si fa una Cadenza, ma s'attacca subito il seguente.*

EE 6862

96

98

534
Fl. 1 2
p
Ob. 1 2
p
Cl. (B♭) 1 2
p
Fg. 1 2
p
Cor. (E♭) 1 2
Tr. (E♭) 1 2
Timp.
[Solo]
ff
Pfte.
Ped.
I
Vl.
II
p
p
Vla.
p
Vc.
Cb.
p

106

EE 6862

108

114

EE 6862

118

120

124

EE 6862

126

EE 6862

III. Rondo

Allegro ma non troppo

EE 6862

142

157

158

162

172

345
Fl. 1 2
Ob. 1 2
Cl. (B♭) 1 2
Fg. 1 2
Cor. (E♭) 1 2
Tr. (E♭) 1 2
Timp.
Pfte.
Tutti
Solo
p espr.
Vl. I II
Vla.
Vc. Cb.

182

184

194

EE 6862